GEORGE WASHINGTON WAS NOT THE FIRST PRESIDENT!

★★★★★★★★★★★★★★★★★★★★★★★★★★★★★★

and Other CRAZY FACTS about Our Presidents

Parachute Press, Inc.
156 Fifth Avenue
New York, NY 10010

Copyright © 1992 Parachute Press, Inc.

ISBN: 0-938753-68-1

Text by Jean Waricha
Design by Greg Wozney Design, Inc.

Illustration by Terry Kovalcik

First printing: September 1992
Printed in the U.S.A.

GEORGE WASHINGTON WAS NOT THE FIRST PRESIDENT!

★★★★★★★★★★★★★★★★★★★★★★★★★★★★★★

and Other **CRAZY FACTS** about Our Presidents

BY JEAN WARICHA

ILLUSTRATION BY TERRY KOVALCIK

Table of Contents

★★★★★★★★★★★★★★★★★★★★★★★★★★★★★★★★★★★★★★★

THE PRESIDENTS OF THE UNITED STATES AND THEIR TERMS OF OFFICE

1. George Washington . . . 1789–1797
2. John Adams . . . 1797–1801
3. Thomas Jefferson . . . 1801–1809
4. James Madison . . . 1809–1817
5. James Monroe . . . 1817–1825
6. John Quincy Adams . . . 1825–1829
7. Andrew Jackson . . . 1829–1837
8. Martin Van Buren . . . 1837–1841
9. William Henry Harrison . . . 1841
10. John Tyler . . . 1841–1845
11. James K. Polk . . . 1845–1849
12. Zachary Taylor . . . 1849–1850
13. Millard Fillmore . . . 1850–1853
14. Franklin Pierce . . . 1853–1857
15. James Buchanan . . . 1857–1861
16. Abraham Lincoln . . . 1861–1865
17. Andrew Johnson . . . 1865–1869
18. Ulysses S. Grant . . . 1869–1877
19. Rutherford B. Hayes . . . 1877–1881
20. James A. Garfield . . . 1881

21. Chester A. Arthur . . . 1881–1885
22. Grover Cleveland . . . 1885–1889
23. Benjamin Harrison . . . 1889–1893
24. Grover Cleveland . . . 1893–1897
25. William McKinley . . . 1897–1901
26. Theodore Roosevelt . . . 1901–1909
27. William Howard Taft . . . 1909–1913
28. Woodrow Wilson . . . 1913–1921
29. Warren G. Harding . . . 1921–1923
30. Calvin Coolidge . . . 1923–1929
31. Herbert Hoover . . . 1929–1933
32. Franklin Delano Roosevelt . . . 1933–1945
33. Harry S Truman . . . 1945–1953
34. Dwight D. Eisenhower . . . 1953–1961
35. John F. Kennedy . . . 1961–1963
36. Lyndon B. Johnson . . . 1963–1969
37. Richard M. Nixon . . . 1969–1974
38. Gerald R. Ford . . . 1974–1977
39. Jimmy Carter . . . 1977–1981
40. Ronald Reagan . . . 1981–1989
41. George Bush . . . 1989–

By a special ruling of the State Department,
Grover Cleveland is considered both the
twenty–second and twenty–fourth president.

Chapter 1

It Isn't Easy Being President

John Hanson was actually the first president. In 1781, while **George Washington** was still off fighting the Revolutionary War, the thirteen colonies joined together under the Articles of Confederation. John Hanson of Maryland was elected "President of the United States in Congress Assembled."

All that meant was that Hanson was the chairman of the Congress. But after winning at Yorktown, Washington himself sent a letter to Hanson, addressed to the "President of the United States."

President **Andrew Johnson** never went to school. His future wife taught him how to read and write when he was seventeen years old.

Some people say **David Atchison** was president of the United States — for one day. When **Zachary Taylor** was elected, the traditional inauguration date fell on a Sunday. Taylor waited to take the oath of office until Monday. Since the terms of President **James K. Polk** and Vice-president George Dallas were over, and President-elect Taylor hadn't been sworn in yet, Senator David Atchison of Missouri, president pro tem of the Senate, was president for March 4, 1849.

After Americans set up the office of the president in the Constitution, they argued over what to call the president. The Senate suggested "His Highness, the President of the United States of America and Protector of the Rights of the Same." **John Adams** wanted something shorter and snappier: "His Most Benign Highness." Another Founding Father, Benjamin Franklin, suggested "His Mightiness." The House of Representatives, however, went by the Constitution. "President of the United States" would have to do.

People from other countries sometimes made up grand titles for the president. When the ruler of Algiers sent a letter to **James Madison**, this is what he wrote: "His Majesty, the Emperor of America, its adjacent and dependent provinces and coasts and wherever his government may extend, our noble friend, the support of the Kings of the nation of Jesus, the most glorious amongst the princes, elected among many lords and nobles, the happy, the great, the amiable James Madison, Emperor of America."

Just think — nowadays our leaders have to get by with the title "Mr. President."

At least two presidents were arrested while they held office. **Ulysses S. Grant** was arrested for driving a horse and carriage too fast. He sent a letter of commendation for the officer who arrested him.

In 1853, **Franklin Pierce** was arrested and charged with running over an old lady with his carriage, but the charges were dropped.

George Washington is often thought of as a rather cold man. Actually he had a hot temper. During the grim days at

Valley Forge, two soldiers got into an argument outside his headquarters. The annoyed Washington came out and knocked their heads together!

Richard M. Nixon liked to call all the plays. Before Super Bowl VI, Nixon phoned Don Shula, coach of the Miami Dolphins, to recommend a play. The Dolphins tried the play — and it failed.

Clothes are said to "make the man." President **Gerald R. Ford** once modeled men's fashions for *Look* magazine.

President **Jimmy Carter** once wore women's high-button shoes. It happened that his father owned a general store in Archery, Georgia, just outside Jimmy's hometown of Plains. Mr. Carter ordered a large number of women's high-button shoes. When he couldn't sell them, he ordered everyone in his family to wear them. Of course, that included fifteen-year-old Jimmy.

But that's not so bad. **Franklin Delano Roosevelt** wore dresses until he was five years old, and he didn't wear long pants until the age of eight. Believe it or not, those were the fashions for well-to-do kids in the 1880s, when young Franklin was growing up.

Andrew Johnson liked to sew. He made his own clothes. Johnson learned to sew when his parents signed him and his brother over as tailors' helpers. They ran away, and for a while the future president had a ten-dollar reward on his head! A few years later, Johnson set up his own tailor shop in Greeneville, Tennessee.

There are many stories about **George Washington** when he was president. For example, he never shook hands with anyone. He thought shaking hands was beneath the dignity of a president. Instead, George bowed to his guests. Later, however, hand shaking became a popular presidential sport. But President

15

Theodore Roosevelt might hold the hand-shaking record. He once shook 8,513 hands at a White House New Year's Day celebration in 1907.

Ulysses S. Grant hated making speeches. When he was running for president in 1868, he stumbled onto what he considered the perfect speech, which he used on many occasions. Here it is:

"I rise only to say I do not intend to say anything. I thank you for your kind words and your hearty welcome."

In 1948 the Republicans, who dominated Congress, were sure that their candidate, Thomas E. Dewey, would win the presidency. They voted to pay huge sums for the inauguration — $80,000 was set just for building grandstands.

The vote ran very close. When the *Chicago Tribune* went to press, it looked as if Dewey had won, so that's what the newspaper printed — in huge letters on the front page. But they were wrong.

In the most stunning upset in American politics, **Harry S Truman** won the election. The Republicans had to watch their old enemy joyfully hold up the newspaper declaring that Dewey had won — and celebrate with all the money they'd voted for.

Zachary Taylor had always been too busy being a soldier to vote. As an army officer, he moved from state to state and never stayed in one place long enough to become a voter. Although the legal voting age was twenty-one in those days, Taylor didn't vote until he was sixty-two years old.

Harry S Truman's middle name was the letter S. It wasn't a middle initial — it was his middle name. One of young Harry's grandfathers was named Shippe, the other, Solomon. Harry's parents let the S stand for both men.

Millard Fillmore was offered an honorary degree from Oxford University. The degree was written in Latin, and Fillmore declined the honor because he believed no one should accept a degree he or she couldn't read.

Herbert Hoover had a very *high* honor given him before he even became president. In 1920 an astronomer named Johann Palisa named an asteroid for Hoover, who ran the aid program for war-torn Europe. The asteroid Hooveria still orbits the Sun.

George Washington was known for frequent use of swear words, but this didn't stop him from issuing an order that forbade swearing in the U.S. Army.

When **Thomas Jefferson** was president, he would go out and do his own food shopping. So did **William Henry Harrison** — carrying a basket under his arm! Harrison gave up shopping, however, when crowds of people started appearing to gawk at him or ask for favors.

President **Lyndon B. Johnson** was sometimes called "Light Bulb" Johnson, but never to his face. It seems that President Johnson was a penny pincher. He was very concerned about the White House electric bill. So at night Johnson would go around to every room and turn out unneeded lights.

You probably know that being a good speller is important. Well, being a good speller saved a president's career.

When **James A. Garfield** was running for president in 1880, his opponents forged a letter and signed Garfield's name to it. The letter stated that Garfield wanted to replace American workers with cheap Chinese labor. The letter was published.

But Garfield was able to prove that he didn't write it. The letter contained two spelling errors. Since Garfield was known as an excellent speller, he proved himself innocent. James Garfield went on to become the twentieth president.

Would you let a jailbird ride in your inaugural parade? That's what **Theodore Roosevelt** did in 1905. At the time of Roosevelt's second inauguration, the famous Indian raider Geronimo was still imprisoned for terrorizing the southwest back in the 1880s. Roosevelt let Geronimo out of prison for the day to join his parade. The once-feared warrior wore a tall silk hat for the occasion.

Some presidents were very poor. When our tenth president, **John Tyler**, left office, he was so poor that five years after leaving the White House, he couldn't afford to pay a bill for $1.25. He had to wait until he could sell his crop.

When **Thomas Jefferson** died in 1826, all his belongings were sold to pay off his debts. Jefferson's home, the beautiful mansion of Monticello, went to ruin for almost a hundred years. Not until 1923 did work on restoring the house begin.

Although **George Washington** did not take good care of his own teeth, he was very concerned about his horses' teeth. Every morning the grooms in Washington's stables had to brush the teeth of the president's six white horses.

President Leslie King? President Hiram Grant? President Stephen Cleveland? President Thomas Wilson? These names may sound odd, but they all belong to presidents. **Gerald Ford** was born Leslie King, Jr. He changed his name when his stepfather legally adopted him.

Ulysses S. Grant began life as Hiram Ulysses Grant. He hated the fact that his initials spelled "hug." So he called himself Ulysses Hiram Grant. When Ulysses went to West Point in 1839, his congressman mistakenly put his name down as Ulysses Simpson Grant. Young Ulysses decided to stick with that name.

Stephen **Grover Cleveland** and Thomas **Woodrow Wilson** are among several presidents who preferred to be called by their middle name.

Zachary Taylor was several days late acknowledging that he would accept the presidency. Why? Because he refused to pay the ten cents postage due on the letter that was sent to tell him he had won.

It was during **Ulysses S. Grant**'s presidency that the telephone was invented by Alexander Graham Bell. But it didn't come into the White House until four presidents later, when **Grover Cleveland** was president. Cleveland used to answer the phone himself. However, **Calvin Coolidge**, our thirtieth president, refused to use the telephone. No wonder he was known as "silent Cal."

James Garfield, our first left-handed president, was nominated at the Republican Convention in 1880. But he was not the delegates' first choice. In fact, on the first round of votes, not one delegate chose Garfield to be the presidential candidate.

Garfield was ambidextrous and multilingual. He could write Greek with his right hand and Latin with his left hand — at the same time! He frequently amused his staff with this feat.

President **Ulysses S. Grant** could usually be found with a cloud of smoke around his head. He had been a moderate cigar smoker until he became famous as a general during the Civil War. Then people sent him as many as ten thousand cigars. With all those cigars lying around, Grant began to smoke more heavily. He smoked as many as twenty cigars a day in later life.

Woodrow Wilson was labeled a slow learner. He was unable to read until he was nine years old. However, he later went to Johns Hopkins University, where he earned a doctoral degree in history. So far, Wilson is the only president to have earned a Ph.D.

On the other hand, **Harry Truman** claimed he had read all the books in the local library by the age of fifteen.

Truman grew up in Independence, Missouri. Unfortunately, we don't know how many books were in the local library when Truman was fifteen.

Jimmy Carter could top this feat. He claimed he could read 2,000 words per minute with 95 percent comprehension. According to Carter, he read at least three to four books a week along with all of the official papers.

When **Ronald Reagan** was a boy, he worked as a lifeguard in a riverfront recreation park near his hometown of Dixon, Illinois. According to Reagan, he saved seventy-seven persons from drowning.

One day while he was on duty as a lifeguard, he earned a little extra money. A swimmer dropped his false teeth in the river while swimming. Ronald Reagan gladly retrieved them. The swimmer gave the future president a ten-dollar tip.

What do you do after being president of the United States? Some ex-presidents went on serving in the government.

William Howard Taft moved from heading the executive branch to the judicial branch. After losing the presidential election of 1912, he became Chief Justice of the Supreme Court in 1921.

Andrew Johnson was nearly thrown out of the presidency in 1868 because of a bitter disagreement with Congress on how to treat the recaptured rebel states after the Civil War. But the Senate failed to impeach him by just one vote. Seven years later Johnson was back in the Senate — this time as the newly elected senator from Tennessee. Twelve of the thirty-five senators who had voted to impeach him were still serving.

But perhaps the oddest government job for an ex-president was becoming president again. **Grover Cleveland** was elected president in 1884 but lost the election of 1888. Four years later, however, Cleveland was reelected president.

The saddest governmental end for a president must be **John Tyler**'s. The tenth president ended his days in Richmond, Virginia, at the beginning of the Civil War. Tyler was a member of the House of Representatives — of the Confederate States of America, which was staging a rebellion against the other states over slavery. Since Tyler was a rebel, it's no surprise that the United States government made no official announcement of his death. Almost fifty years passed before Congress finally voted funds for a Tyler monument.

John Quincy Adams went skinny-dipping every morning in the Potomac River. His habit was so well known that in 1828 a reporter forced the president to grant her an interview. She sat on top of his clothes lying on the riverbank so he couldn't get away from her — or out of the water — until he answered her questions.

Did you ever wonder where the slang expression "big cheese" comes from? It may date to an odd episode in **Thomas Jefferson**'s presidency.

In January 1802, Jefferson received a 1,235-pound cheese from well-wishers in Pennsylvania. The cheese had arrived in a coach drawn by six horses and was inscribed, "The greatest cheese in America, for the greatest man in America." Thomas Jefferson always refused to accept any gifts, but the cheese was so huge that sending it back would have cost the government a fortune. Jefferson kept the cheese but paid for it with his own money.

Some years later, in 1835, **Andrew Jackson** received an even bigger cheese. A New York dairy farmer sent a four-foot-wide, 1,400-pound cheddar cheese to the White House. Jackson kept the cheese but made it available to the public. Hundreds of people flocked to Washington to get a piece of free cheese. And for years afterward, the White House smelled of cheese.

John Quincy Adams is, so far, the only son of a president to also become president.

Benjamin Harrison, our twenty-third president, was the grandson of **William Henry Harrison**, the ninth president.

Franklin Delano Roosevelt and **Teddy Roosevelt** were fifth cousins.

Every president has his own distinctive signature — usually one that's impossible to read. One reason could be that a president sometimes signs his name to an official document with several different pens. He does this so he can give away the pens as souvenirs.

President **Franklin Delano Roosevelt** used ten different pens to sign the Guffey Coal Control bill, legislation for miners' labor rights, which was later found unconstitutional. Others say he once used as many as thirty different pens to sign another bill. Good thing he had such a long name.

Chapter 2

Funny Facts About First Families

Dolley Madison, wife of President **James Madison**, was trying to redecorate the White House and bought a new mirror.

The Senate found out that the mirror was imported — a political no-no in the early 1800s. The senators were so upset about Dolley Madison's wasting American money on foreign goods that they launched an investigation to find out the cost of the mirror. They found out that the mirror cost $40, but their investigation cost $2,000.

When President **Lyndon B. Johnson** went to Samoa, a native chief offered him kava, the ceremonial drink of the island. Worried that it would make Johnson sick, the Secret Service wouldn't let him drink it.

Instead, they gave the kava to someone who was "expendable," someone who could "afford" to get sick. **Lady Bird Johnson**, the first lady, was the one who drank the kava.

Whenever you see pictures of **Ulysses S. Grant**'s wife, **Julia Grant**, she sits with one side to the camera. Julia was cross-eyed. She wanted to try a newly developed operation to correct her problem. Grant changed her mind. He said, "I like your eyes crossed."

Mary Todd Lincoln was known as a compulsive shopper. When she went shopping, she liked to buy enormous quantities of expensive merchandise. In a three-month period she bought three hundred pairs of gloves. At one time she spent $27,000 on dresses, shawls, and hats. Even today that's a pretty hefty sum. But in the 1860s it was a fabulous amount of money. The average salary was less than $10 a week.

Jane Means Appleton married **Franklin Pierce**, America's fourteenth president, when he was in Congress. The couple had three sons—two died in infancy. Mrs. Pierce became terribly depressed.

When her husband was nominated for president, she asked him to decline. She begged him to give up politics. She prayed that he would lose.

But Pierce won. Soon after—but before he became president—he and his family were on a train ride when a terrible accident occurred and their only living son, Benjamin, was killed before their eyes.

Mrs. Pierce didn't attend her husband's inauguration. She wore black every day she lived in the White House.

Abigail Smith Adams, wife of **John Adams**, was often criticized for running her husband's affairs. Some called her Mrs. President. But Mrs. Adams didn't care what people said — even about the family's private affairs. She created quite a commotion in early Washington by stringing clotheslines in the unfinished East Room of the White House to dry the family laundry.

During the presidency of **Rutherford B. Hayes**, Congress decided to do away with the annual Easter egg hunt, which was held in front of the Capitol. They said it was ruining the national lawn. **Lucy Hayes**, the first lady, had the activity moved to the White House lawn, which began the White House egg hunt tradition.

When widower **Woodrow Wilson** married his second wife, he was marrying a lot of American history. **Edith Bolling Wilson** was descended from John Rolfe, one of the first English settlers in America, and his wife Pocahontas, the Indian princess who saved John Smith's life. As first lady, Mrs. Wilson often christened ships with Indian names.

Martha Washington gave wonderful parties in Philadelphia when **George Washington** was president. Everyone invited attended. However, they always ended at 9:00 P.M. That was Mrs. Washington's bedtime.

Julia Tyler, wife of President **John Tyler**, loved jewelry. She sometimes wore a forehead jewel, which hung from a strand of pearls. When her husband died, she wanted to find just the right jewelry to wear. She finally decided that a piece of coal, cut and polished to look like a gem, would be the perfect jewelry for a funeral.

Martin Van Buren probably loved his wife very much. He was married to her for twelve years before she died, and together they had four sons. But when President Van Buren wrote his autobiography, he never mentioned **Hannah Hoes Van Buren**, his lovely wife—not even once.

Grace Coolidge, **Calvin Coolidge**'s wife, was worried that her sons wouldn't learn how to play baseball because the president was too busy to teach them. So Mrs. Coolidge learned to pitch, catch, and bat, and played ball on the White House lawn with the boys.

Jimmy and Rosalynn Carter often asked their daughter, Amy, to dine with them on official state occasions. Amy was ten years old when her father became president. What does a young girl do when she's at a long state dinner? While the president of Mexico was dining at the White House, Amy was reading a Nancy Drew mystery between courses.

William McKinley was very devoted to his wife, **Ida McKinley**, who suffered from epilepsy. The illness did not stop her from being the White House hostess, however. At official dinners she would always sit next to Mr. McKinley. If she lapsed into unconsciousness, her husband would put a handkerchief over her face until she recovered.

Eleanor Roosevelt was a terrible cook. Once she served the king of England hot dogs for dinner.

Betty Ford was plump as a child. In the summer her family lived at a cottage near a lake and Betty would wander off to nearby picnic grounds. She would go from one table to the next, and everyone would offer her a cookie or some cake. Since Betty was getting fatter and fatter, her mother finally hung a sign on her back: PLEASE DO NOT FEED THIS CHILD.

Abraham Lincoln's son Tad had a secret code with his father. Three quick knocks followed by two slow ones always got him into his father's office, no matter what important meetings were going on. "I promised never to go back on the code," Lincoln said.

When the **Kennedys** entertained in the White House, they allowed three-year-old Caroline to watch the adults from the grand staircase. On one occasion the Marine Band noticed little Caroline sitting on the staircase. After they played "Hail to the Chief," the Marine Band played "Old MacDonald Had a Farm."

Alice Roosevelt was the oldest daughter of **Theodore Roosevelt**. Alice, who was given the nickname "Princess Alice," was a free spirit and did just about anything she wanted to do. She especially liked to shock her parents, the press, or any White House guests.

Once she attended a White House dinner wearing long white kid leather gloves. When asparagus was served, she proceeded to pick up stalks with her fingers — without taking off her gloves.

Another time Alice attended a party for diplomats. Alice sat next to a woman who constantly talked about her poor health. Alice sat and listened to the woman's description of each and every ache and pain. Then Alice said to the woman, "Have you ever tried standing on your head?" With that, Alice jumped up, pinned her skirt together between her knees, and stood on her head.

"Great exercise," Alice said with perfect composure. After a few seconds, Alice stood upright, took her seat, and had a cup of tea.

As Theodore Roosevelt said of his daughter, "I can be president of the United States, or I can control Alice. I cannot possibly do both."

In 1906, Alice married Congressman Nicholas Longworth. Their wedding was the social event of the year.

No expense was too great. The White House was decorated with gold-rimmed cloth. Ropes of lilies hung from the walls. Persian rugs lined the floors.

After the ceremony, Alice began to cut the cake, but the knife was too dull. She tried again. Finally, frustrated at her efforts, she turned to an army major nearby and politely asked for his dress sword.

Alice took the sword, raised it over her head, and began slashing at the cake. Within minutes everyone had a piece.

Chapter 3

Here's Looking at You

Theodore Roosevelt led the Rough Riders in the Spanish-American War in 1898. However, good ole Teddy had very bad eyesight, and he was always afraid of losing his glasses in battle. To prevent this from happening, Roosevelt always took along at least half a dozen extra pairs.

He had these sewn into his clothes, tucked into his hat, and stuffed into his pockets.

All **the presidents** have had to wear glasses — although not all of them wore glasses in public.

President **Ulysses S. Grant** wore false teeth. When he was in the army, he put his teeth into a washstand overnight. A servant girl accidentally threw them out in the morning when she dumped the washbowl into the river. Grant sent for a new pair, but until they arrived he couldn't eat solid food.

Another famous false-teeth wearer was **George Washington**. His imitation choppers were made from cows' teeth, hippopotamus teeth, elephant ivory, and even other human teeth. The false teeth were held in place by the one tooth Washington had left in his mouth. He lived in fear of losing that single tooth!

During his second term, **Grover Cleveland** developed cancer of the mouth. Doctors were forced to remove most of his left jaw and fitted the president with an artificial one made out of vulcanized rubber.

John Quincy Adams didn't care much about clothes, supposedly wearing the same hat for ten years.

In 1813, **Andrew Jackson** got into a fight with the Benton brothers. Jackson was shot, and the bullet was trapped in his shoulder. Doctors feared that an attempt to dislodge the bullet would cripple Jackson, so they left the bullet undisturbed. After twenty years of pain, Jackson asked a surgeon to remove the bullet. By this time Jackson was president, and Thomas Hart Benton was a senator. The bullet was removed, and Jackson offered it to Benton, who was now a friend. Benton suggested that Jackson should keep it, having carried it around longer.

Franklin Delano Roosevelt once gave one of his Secret Service guards a crash course in impersonating the president while riding on a train. He gave the guard a pair of his trademark glasses, his cigarette holder, and told the man to wave and smile out the window whenever the train passed through a town. Roosevelt would have done it himself, but he wanted to take a nap.

James Madison was the smallest chief executive. He stood only five feet four inches tall and weighed less than a hundred pounds.

One American president was so big he couldn't fit into the White House bathtub. **William Howard Taft** was six feet tall and weighed more than three hundred pounds. After getting stuck in the tub, he had a giant-sized one put in. How big was the new tub? The four plumbers who installed it celebrated by having their picture taken — while they were all sitting inside it.

Taft tried to lose weight. He exercised and dieted but had little success. Before he was president, Taft was governor general of the Philippines. After a brief illness, Taft received a cable from Elihu Root, the secretary of war. Root asked if Taft felt better. Taft replied that he felt great. He had just gone for a twenty-five-mile horseback ride. His friend Root then inquired, "How's the horse?"

Taft frequently joked about his size. Once when he was offered a "Chair of Law at Yale," Taft said that he would need a "sofa" instead of a "chair" because of his weight.

Other presidents were also concerned about their weight. **Richard Nixon** tried to lose weight by eating cottage cheese and ketchup for lunch. **Lyndon Johnson** desserted on low-calorie tapioca.

Presidents are often said to leave "a mighty big pair of shoes" for their successors to fill. Well, some presidents did have mighty big feet. **Abraham Lincoln** and **Warren G. Harding** both wore size fourteen shoes. **George Washington** wore size thirteen boots.

Zachary Taylor was a hero of the Mexican War. But he hardly looked like a hero. He had a large head but a stumpy body. He hardly looked like a general, either. Taylor liked to wear baggy pants, a long coat without any badges of rank, and a broad-brimmed farmer's hat.

Once a young lieutenant came up to the shabbily dressed general, calling him an old codger — only to discover he was talking to his commanding officer!

President **William Howard Taft** was so tone deaf that he could not recognize the national anthem. When it was played, someone would have to tap him so he would know to stand up.

Portraits of six presidents can be found on coins. The **Eisenhower** silver dollar, first issued in 1971, is the most recent coin portrait of a deceased president.

Other coin portraits include the **Kennedy** half dollar, the **Jefferson** nickel, the **Washington** quarter, the **Lincoln** penny, and the **Roosevelt** dime.

An eleven-year-old girl from Westfield, New York, saw a photo of **Abraham Lincoln** when he was running for president in 1860 and wrote to suggest that he would look better with a beard. While on the way to be inaugurated in Washington, Lincoln stopped off in Westfield to show the girl, Grace Bedell, his new whiskers.

James Polk was not a big man, and often wasn't noticed when he came in for White House parties. His wife got the idea of announcing the president's arrival by playing an old Scottish song — "Hail to the Chief." Ever since, presidents have made entrances to that song's ruffles and flourishes.

Chapter 4

White House Follies

Thomas Jefferson often entertained in the White House. He spared no expense on the food. However, he hated dressing up and frequently wore his bathrobe and slippers to dinner parties.

When **Herbert Hoover** and his wife didn't want the servants in the White House to know what they were saying, they spoke to each other in Chinese.

When presidents leave the White House, they usually take their personal belongings with them. When Edith Roosevelt, wife of **Teddy Roosevelt**, left the White House, she had the bodies of the dead family pets dug up and taken to their house at Sagamore Hill, New York.

When **Millard Fillmore** moved into the White House, there wasn't a book in the place — not even a Bible. Thanks to his wife's insistence, Congress voted funds for a White House library. As set up by Mrs. Fillmore, it was considered the nicest room in the Fillmore White House.

Sometimes the White House staff makes a blunder despite their efforts to make every occasion special. One time Queen Elizabeth visited the White House during the presidency of **Gerald Ford**. At a reception dance Ford whisked the queen onto the dance floor. The two danced while the band played "The Lady Is a Tramp."

Thomas Jefferson was the second president to live in the White House, but he didn't like the place.

Jefferson called it "a great stone house, big enough for two emperors, one pope, and the grand lama in the bargain." Perhaps Jefferson's dislike was because he himself had submitted a design under the name Abraham Faws. Jefferson's design came in second to Irish-born architect James Hoban. But there were other things to dislike about the early White House. When Jefferson took office in 1801, the only bathroom in the executive mansion was an outhouse.

James Buchanan didn't like the White House either. He refused to stay there in the summer months, fearing diseases from the nearby swamps. During his stay in the late 1850s, Buchanan incorrectly predicted that presidents would no longer live in the White House, but only use it as an office.

When **Jimmy and Rosalynn Carter** lived in the White House, they were especially careful to watch their spending. If members of Congress were invited over for a bacon and egg breakfast, the Carters sent each a bill for $4.75.

The Carters were so frugal that they spent only $1,372 of the $50,000 annual budget they were allowed for entertainment expenses.

The White House has often been repaired and redecorated. Furniture, lamps, desks, beds, and tables have been loaded up and dumped many times.

But when **Harry Truman** moved in, the White House was in really sad shape. The piano of Truman's daughter, Margaret, put a leg through the upstairs floor — shared with the dining-room ceiling below. Years of boring for gas pipes and electrical wires had weakened the whole structure. So the White House was repaired and rebuilt once again. But this time Truman decided that all the "junk" was to be sold as souvenirs. Even odd pieces of wood were made into gavels and sold to souvenir hunters.

When **Chester A. Arthur** became the twenty-first president in 1881, he achieved the dream of many Americans. But for him the White House was no dream house. He refused to move in until all the old furniture was auctioned off. Once the old stuff was gotten rid of, he redecorated with all new furniture — new furniture in an old style, a style designed a hundred years earlier.

Warren G. Harding was our twenty-ninth president, from 1921 to 1923. He frequently played poker when he was in the White House. One night he gambled and lost an entire set of White House china that dated back to the 1740s.

Lots of presidents kept traditional kinds of pets in the White House. But **Thomas Jefferson** kept a pet mockingbird in his White House study. For fun he taught the bird to take food from his mouth.

During World War I, **Woodrow and Edith Wilson** did everything they could to help the war effort — including keeping a herd of sheep on the White House lawn. The sheep ate the grass, so the Wilsons didn't need a groundskeeper. Furthermore, the sheep were shorn and the wool was sold. The flock brought in more than $100,000, which the Wilsons donated to the Red Cross.

Lyndon B. Johnson kept his pet dogs at the White House. When the president's favorite dog, Old Beagle, died, Johnson had the hound cremated. The ashes were put in a box and kept on top of the refrigerator until the president decided on their final resting place.

For Yuki, another Johnson dog, special plastic boots were made for walks in the rain.

But Johnson upset pet lovers in 1964, when he was photographed picking up another beagle, Him, by the dog's floppy ears.

One of the most famous pets in the White House was Fala, **Franklin Delano Roosevelt**'s dog. Fala went wherever Roosevelt went.

One summer in 1944, Fala and the president went on a cruise to Hawaii. Fala would disappear for hours. His hair appeared to be falling out. The president was worried.

An investigation was begun to find out where Fala was going. As it turned out, the ship's crew members had been feeding Fala leftovers while they clipped off pieces of the dog's hair for souvenirs. President Roosevelt quickly put an end to that practice.

William McKinley kept a pet parrot that could whistle "Yankee Doodle."

William Howard Taft kept a cow on the White House lawn so he could have fresh milk.

Zachary Taylor rode off to the Mexican War on a horse named Old Whitey. When Taylor was elected president in 1848, Old Whitey came to the White House, too — spending his days eating the grass on the White House lawn. White House visitors would pull hairs from the horse's tail as souvenirs. When Taylor died after only sixteen months in office, Old Whitey's tail was nearly bald!

Many presidents have always been big eaters, as you might suspect from the first line of **Martha Washington's** favorite recipe: "Take fifty eggs. . ."

Some presidents had odd tastes in food. **Andrew Jackson** loved to start his day with a breakfast of turkey hash on waffles.

Thomas Jefferson was perhaps the most adventurous eater in the White House. Many foods he "discovered" while serving as ambassador in Europe (France) have become American favorites. Jefferson introduced French fries, pasta, and parmesan cheese to America.

Teddy Roosevelt was a steak lover — it was his favorite food, especially when cooked rare. **Lyndon B. Johnson** had special steaks for barbecues at the LBJ Ranch. The meat was cut in the shape of Texas.

And what about vegetables? Sadly, presidents don't have a good record on eating greens.

Everyone has heard how President **George Bush** hates broccoli. But he's not the only president who has had strong feelings about vegetables. In 1933 a ten-year-old boy went with his parents for lunch at the White House and was served spinach. His friends didn't believe him, so the boy wrote to President **Herbert Hoover**, asking the president to back him up. Hoover sent the boy this note:

"We indeed had spinach at the White House," Hoover wrote, "and I don't like it either. Mrs. Hoover makes me eat it."

Chapter 5

Presidential
Firsts

Dwight D. Eisenhower was the first president to use makeup for TV appearances.

John Tyler was the first vice-president to take office because the elected president (William Henry Harrison) died. Tyler was also the first president to remarry in office — and the first to face a serious threat of impeachment.

Tyler also holds the presidential record for having the most children. He fathered eight children by his first wife and seven by his second. The life span of his fifteen children from the birth of his first to the death of his last was 131 years.

Electricity was first installed in the White House in 1890, during the presidency of **Benjamin Harrison.** Electric lights should have modernized the White House and been a wonderful improvement. The Harrisons, however, were afraid to turn them on. The lights had to be turned on and off by servants.

Jimmy Carter was the first president to be born in a hospital. That happened on October 1, 1924.

William Howard Taft was the first president to kick off the baseball season by throwing out the first ball. He started the custom back in 1910.

Martin Van Buren was the eighth president of the United States. But he was the first president to be born an American citizen. Van Buren was born in 1782, six years after the Declaration of Independence was signed.

The last president to be born a British subject was Van Buren's successor, **William Henry Harrison**. He was born on February 9, 1773, while Virginia was still a British colony. His father, Benjamin Harrison, was a signer of the Declaration of Independence.

James Monroe was the first president to ride on a steamship.

The first log-cabin president was **Andrew Jackson**. In the 1800s, Americans loved to vote for candidates who had been born in log cabins. It meant the candidate came from the frontier. And since a log cabin was also a humble home, it showed how an American with modest beginnings could still lead the country. The best-loved log-cabin president was **Abraham Lincoln**. **William Henry Harrison** pretended he'd been born in a log cabin, and was elected president in 1840. But the last log-cabin candidate was Alben Barkley, who ran for vice-president on **Harry Truman**'s presidential ticket in 1948.

The first assassination attempt on a president occurred in 1835. A crazy man named Richard Lawrence fired two pistols at close range at President **Andrew Jackson**. Lawrence believed he was king of America and had to kill Jackson to regain his throne. Neither of Lawrence's guns fired. Lawrence spent the rest of his life in an insane asylum.

Richard Nixon was the first president to resign from office — on August 9, 1974.

Because of Nixon's resignation, **Gerald Ford** became the first (and so far only) president who took office without an election. Ford was a member of the House of Representatives when **Nixon** and his vice-president, Spiro Agnew, were reelected in 1972. On October 10, 1973, Agnew resigned the vice-presidency during his trial on tax-evasion charges. Nixon nominated Ford under the provisions of the Twenty-fifth Amendment to the Constitution, and Ford was sworn in as vice-president on December 6, 1973. Less than a year later, Ford became the thirty-eighth president.

Incidentally, **Nixon** was not the first president to serve without a vice-president. **Franklin Pierce** lost his vice-president only six weeks into his term of office. Pierce and his running mate, William Rufus DeVane King, won the 1852 election. King was sworn in as vice-president on March 4, 1853, while he was visiting Cuba. He was the first and only person to take the oath of office outside the United States. On April 18, 1853, King died of a sudden illness.

While most people consider the vice-presidency a do-nothing job, that was especially true in King's case. He never got to preside over the Senate, which is the only job given the vice-president in the Constitution.

Woodrow Wilson was the first president to cross the Atlantic while in office. In 1918 he sailed for France to help write the treaty that ended World War I.

Eleanor Roosevelt was the first first lady to vote in a presidential election. In 1920 women won the right to vote with the passage of the Nineteenth Amendment to the Constitution. In the 1920 election, Eleanor's husband **Franklin Roosevelt** was running for vice-president. He lost.

Thirteen years later, he became our thirty-second president, and Eleanor became the first lady.

The oldest man to be president was **Ronald Reagan**. He was sixty-nine years old when he was elected.

Our youngest president was **Theodore Roosevelt** — he was forty-two when he took office. The next youngest was **John F. Kennedy**, who was forty-six. According-ing to the U.S. Constitution, presidents must be at least thirty-five years old.

John Adams was the first president to live in the White House. He moved in on November 1, 1800. When John and Abigail Adams headed for Washington, the nation's capital was a small town of 3,000 people. Washington was sur-rounded by forests, and the Adamses got lost in the woods for two hours.

Calvin Coolidge was the first — and so far only — president born on the Fourth of July. That was in 1872. He was named John Calvin Coolidge.

Andrew Jackson was the first candidate to win the most popular votes and the most electoral votes — and still lose the election.

In 1824, Jackson ran in a four-cornered contest with **John Quincy Adams**, William Harris Crawford, and Henry Clay. Jackson had the most votes, nearly 40 percent of the total. But the election went to the House of Representatives, where Clay's supporters went over to Adams.

Jackson lost that time around, but four years later he defeated Adams, with 68 percent of the vote.

Tricia Nixon, daughter of **Richard Nixon**, was the first person to be married in an outdoor ceremony in the White House Rose Garden — and it rained.

Warren G. Harding was the first president who knew how to drive a car.

Thomas Jefferson was the first president to grow a tomato in North America. In the early 1800s, Americans were afraid of tomatoes. They thought they were poisonous.

Chapter 6

The End(s)

George Washington died on December 14, 1799, at the age of sixty-seven. He left a handwritten will. Washington was a fanatic about neatness and penmanship. His will consisted of fifteen sheets of parchment marked with his personal monogram, numbered, signed, and with every line exactly the same length.

Washington died an agonizingly slow and painful death. In fact, his doctors probably killed him with their ineptness. Two days before his death, Washington went horseback riding in bad weather. As a result, he developed a sore throat. He called the doctor.

The practice of medicine was not a science in the 1700s. Germ theory was years in the future, and "cures" using cow manure, applied to the outside of the cheek, were common for problems like tooth aches or colds. Another well intentioned but seriously flawed medical practice of the day was drawing blood to stop inflammations. Washington was bled for his sore throat and fever. On the day he died, he'd been severely weakened by losing a quart of blood.

Since Washington feared being buried alive, his body was not put into the vault until two days after he was pronounced dead.

Ulysses S. Grant, who smoked cigars, died of throat cancer on July 23, 1885. His last spoken word was "water."

William Henry Harrison died on April 4, 1841. He had the shortest presidency in history, only thirty-one days. He was also the first president to die in office.

Harrison caught pneumonia while giving his two-hour inaugural address in freezing, stormy weather. He refused to wear a hat, scarf, coat, or boots. Later that night, although suffering from chills and sweats, he danced at three separate parties. One month later he was dead.

His widow was paid a year's presidential salary, $25,000, as a pension. She lived on for more than thirty years after Harrison's death.

Everyone dreams — including presidents. But in 1865, **Abraham Lincoln** had a dream that upset him very much.

By early April of 1865, Lincoln had gotten many threats of assassination. In fact, he had collected eighty threatening letters. They didn't worry him, but the dream he had worried him so much he had to tell his wife and a close friend about it. The friend wrote the story down.

In his dream Lincoln saw himself walking through the White House. He heard sounds of sobbing and followed the noise to the East Room of the White House, where he met a young soldier.

"Why is everyone weeping?" Lincoln asked.

"The president has been assassinated. He's dead," answered the soldier.

A loud roar of grief woke the president up. Although Lincoln knew it was just a dream, he could not forget it. It haunted him until his death a few days later — when he was killed by John Wilkes Booth.

Zachary Taylor died on July 9, 1850, at the age of sixty-five. He was the only president to die of sunstroke.

July 4, 1850, was an unusually hot and humid day. On that day Taylor attended the ceremony to lay the cornerstone for the Washington Monument. He wore a black suit with a high white starched collar. During the ceremony, he started to sweat and became flushed. Feeling faint, he drank a whole pitcher of water that had been left out in the sun for two hours.

Later that afternoon he developed chills, sweats, and became ravenously hungry. He ate a large bowl of strawberries and cherries. Within an hour he was doubled over with cramps and collapsed. Within days of that he was dead. Doctors think Taylor might have died of cholera, picked up from the water or the fruit, but the official cause of death is listed as sunstroke. He was the second president to die in office.

Franklin D. Roosevelt died on April 12, 1945, of a massive cerebral hemorrhage. After he was buried, his wife Eleanor found a letter with his two last requests — not to be embalmed and not to have a Washington procession. Neither request had been followed.

When Eleanor died in 1962, she, too, requested not to be embalmed, and she wasn't. But Eleanor feared being buried alive, so as she requested, she had her major veins severed so there would be no chance she wasn't dead.

The fiftieth anniversary of the Declaration of Independence was a sad day for many Americans. Two of the most famous signers passed away that day.

John Adams died on July 4, 1826, at the age of ninety. He was one of the healthiest presidents and the only one to reach ninety years and 200 days. He died of natural causes at home. His last words were "**Thomas Jefferson** still survives."

Although Thomas Jefferson wrote the

Declaration and John Adams fought for its passage, the two men later became bitter political opponents who ran against each other for the presidency in 1800. Little did Adams know that Thomas Jefferson had actually died before him. Jefferson died at 9:50 that same morning, at the age of eighty-three.

The fact that two former presidents died on July Fourth created quite a stir. Some predicted that the end of the world was near. They were wrong.

Woodrow Wilson died on February 3, 1924. But Wilson had been sick since 1919, when a stroke all but crippled him. For the last year and a half of Wilson's term, First Lady Edith Wilson ran the White House and kept the president's condition a secret.

All matters of importance had to be submitted in writing to the first lady. She would take them to the president and appear later with his "wishes." Edith Wilson actually made all the decisions and even forged his name.

Woodrow Wilson did not run in the 1920 election because of his ill health. **Warren G. Harding**, ten years younger, was elected president. Harding died in 1923, while still in his first term. Wilson died in 1924.

The presidencies of **Abraham Lincoln**, **James Garfield**, and **John F. Kennedy** were all ended by assassin's bullets. In 1912, while running for president on the Bull Moose ticket, **Theodore Roosevelt**'s life was nearly brought to an end. A crazed would-be assassin fired a gun right into Roosevelt's chest. Roosevelt's life was saved by his eyeglass case, and by the fifty-page speech folded up in his jacket pocket. The bullet did enter his chest, but it had been slowed so that the wound wasn't fatal.

Although he was bleeding, Roosevelt went on to make a fifty-minute speech. "I have just been wounded," he told his audience. "But it takes more than that to kill a Bull Moose."